Science and Our Words

Do We Need a Moon-Shot Project
For Our People-Based Words?

Loran Joly

Contents

Chapter One

Are We More "Scientific" Today in ALL Areas or Only SOME Areas?

IF we SAY we are NOW in the SCIENTIFIC era, are the WORDS, and IF we say we are MAKING PROGRESS, as a SPECIES, are ALL of our WORDS – our TERMS - MATCHING this claim?

Or are SOME of the words – the TERMS – which we presently have, quite UN-SCIENTIF-IC, still?

***

I am particularly referring to the words we have, at our "disposal" – in DICTIONARIES – for aspects of PEOPLE.

And surely,

JUST like ROCKET SCIENCE and OTH-ER COMPLEX Modern-day areas REQUIRES CALCULUS - INCLUDING Calulus-based TERMS, SO TOO does the DISCUSSING of PEOPLE-Topics, REQUIRE a SET of TERMS, IF to be PERMANENT-based terms, NOT terms that are EPHEMORAL, e.g. TRANSITORY, such as FEELINGS or "IMPRESSIONS" or "IN-TUITIONS".

TERMS that are USEFUL-Enough to be HELPFUL, and SUITABLE, thus.

One might call these, GOOD-ENOUGH terms, or GOOD-ENOUGH TOOLS, even, "Scientific" terms, IF one were desiring to use THIS term:

Where perhaps, Science is not just about Hypothesis-Testing, but moreover, SOUND LOGIC.

Including SOUND LOGIC as BUILT INTO the very TOOLS utilized: its WORD-SET.

***

SIMILARLY, the CONSTRUCTING of a HOME, or the repairing of a CAR, requires such terms: such TOOLS, galore, too.

They thus need NOMENCLATURE. NAMES. TERMS.

And the NAME of such tools surely ought to be LOGICALLY SOUND: when we want to use a HAMMER, we are counting on that hammer BEING a hammer, and NOT a NAIL or a SAW, even IF all of these tools ARE, in fact, made out of METAL.

We want ALL crucial aspects of that tool to meet our needs, NOT just the aspect of it being made of METAL.

Chapter Two

Do Our PEOPLE-Words have an "UN-SCIENTIFIC" (Irrational) SLANT?

Is there a key issue, with our Words, then?

IS there a PROBLEM with our TOOLS, our WORDS – when we are DISCUSSING PEOPLE?

Do the terms we use – the tools – have certain "SLANTS", certain BUILT-IN ERRORS – all too often – which in essence result in providing some POSITIVE results, but also, some NEGATIVE results?

DO our PEOPLE-words state SOME aspects of people CORRECTLY, but NOT some OTHER aspects of such words?

Just like a SAW is made of METAL, but we may have WANTED a tool that was a HAMMER, ALSO made out of metal, but having OTHER aspects.

***

Now, when it comes to PEOPLE, and PEOPLE-related tools, or as I call such, PEOPLE-Based WORDS, I have been working, for years, on this question:

ARE our PEOPLE-based TERMS – our PEOPLE-words, CONTAMINATED with something, as if we are then TALKING to ourselves and others while, at the same time, spreading a COMMUNICABLE HEALTH problem?

Yes, do our PEOPLE-words have some BENEFITS of a surgeon's SCALPEL, but a scalpel that has NOT been SANITIZED, and has many toxic GERMS which can cause pains?

Chapter Three

Are There Three Types of Words?

Object-Words, Money-Words, and People-Words

I would submit, that Mankind is NOT YET UNIVERSALLY ACKNOWLEDGING that PEOPLE (HUMANS), do indeed follow the Laws of the Universe: that we are NOT EXEMPT from The Universe's set of CAUSE and EFFECT relationships.

***

And, because many of us can sometimes find it UNPLEASANT to have to admit that some things will NEVER CHANGE, or will TAKE TIME to change, or this change would perhaps be UN-PREDICTABLE, in HOW it would happen, we DON'T LIKE to SEE that WE TOO have some-thing in COMMON with NON-Humans: with Objects, even, or Money:

That ALL Matter in the Universe – including the Matter that is called "HUMAN BEING-Mat-ter" – is SUBJECT to The Laws of The Universe, and NOT "Wishful Thinking", aka FREE WILL, as philosophers talk of:

Or as Einstein believed, "God Does Not Play Dice With the Universe" (ANY PART of the Uni-verse, whether "Objects", or Money, or PEOPLE, even).

Chapter Four

Are People-Words Structured DIFFERENTLY Than The OTHER TWO Types of Words?

Are People-Words Free-Will Oriented, Whereas Object and Money Words are Deterministic Oriented?

So, if Mankind is often stressed, and under such times, in particular, would like to see this stress, this pain, we might say, REDUCED, and also NEVER HAPPEN AGAIN, it strikes me that we would find ourselves at times, very comforted, IF we can only believe we can *MAGICALLY* CHANGE things:

***

And what better way of such magic, than to believe that ANYTHING can HAPPEN, anything CHANGE, without the NEEDED RE-SOURCES and FREEDOM from certain CON-STRAINTS.

That we can BAKE a CAKE, without ANY IN-GREDIENTS needed. Simply FANTASY-ingre-dients.

Hence, "enter" the Words of Mankind, regarding PEOPLE:

And my growing view, solid-enough but not 100% so in certainty, that there is the following:

***

That the WORD-SET used to discuss PEO-PLE, is UTTERLY DIFFERENT, in "philo-sophical underpinnings", that the word-sets for NON-Peoples ("Objects"): including machines or Money, even.

Chapter Five

Some Say That Free-Will Seems to Provide Us With HOPE?

I propose that The WORD-SET for both "IN-animate", and MONEY-related, ENTITIES, are DETERMINISTIC.

But, that the WORD-SET for PEOPLE, is utterly, and I do mean, UTTERLY, oriented, still, toward FREE WILL.

Why? Because Free Will, and the VOCABU-LARY we USE, regarding People, gives us a sense that we, others, and situations in general, can AL-WAYS CHANGE, and EASILY, too.

And so, it seemingly provides us HOPE, for the alleviating of PAINS, in life, in particular.

QUICKLY, too. And ALWAYS.

***

Put another way, it reflects a desire and belief, that we can always "HAVE OUR CAKE AND EAT IT TOO": that we can HAVE WHATEVER WE WANT, ALWAYS, and QUICKLY, too, IF we CAN obtain it.

It is perhaps, thus, a (MAGIC) PILLor (MAG-IC) WAND, for NOT FACING our LIMITA-TIONS: our LIMITATIONS in terms of both our RESOURCES, and IMMUTABLE CON-

STRAINTS, at least for a WHILE, to include, while we are alive, perhaps.

***

For, through FREE WILL, we get to say, "LIM-ITATIONS do NOT, in fact, EXIST"!

That ANYTHING is POSSIBLE, without the needed RESOURCES and freedom from xyz CONSTRAINTS, too.

In other words, that we CAN have "WHATEV-ER we WANT, and WHEN we want it".

Hence, phrases such as, "Where there's a WILL (or DESIRE), there's a WAY".

Or, "You can HAVE WHATEVER your mind can CONCEIVE".

Or, that we can be "SELF-MADE" Men and Women.

***

As opposed to being UTTERLY "MADE" by a CHAIN of PRIOR EVENTS, which one could call "The RESOURCES and CONSTRAINTS which are essentially WHO we ARE.

Chapter Six

Free Will Says We Can BE WHATEVER We DESIRE

Free Will says ANYONE Can Become an ASTRONAUT or PRESIDENT or BILLIONAIRE or even LIVE TEN BILLION YEARS

A curiosity, I find, regarding Free Will and Determinism, or what I call the differing claims that ANYTHING can be, vs ONLY what The Laws of the Universe CONSTRAIN things to be, is this:

That, while PHILOSOPHERS have, for eons, discussed whether FREE WILL or DETERMIN-ISM is TRUE,

AND, further, that a SMALLER number who SAY that they BELIEVE in DETERMINISM,

YET, I nevertheless do not believe I am seeing any significant discussion, yet, of how we apparently can still have a TREMENDOUS "DISCON-NECT", between CLAIMING to believe in Determinism, yet NOT believe in it, in SOME OTH-ER way.

***

NOT believing in Determinism – for PEOPLE – when it comes down to the NITTY GRITTY.

***

The NITTY GRITTY of our WORDS.

Chapter Seven

Almost EVERY People-Word in DICTIONARIES May Well be a FREE-WILL WORD

Thus, it appears to me, that it is possible to believe in Determinism, we CLAIM, and with regard to People, too, and yet, at the SAME time, NOT believe it: not when it comes to the actual WORDS we UTILIZE, our PEOPLE-words.

Hence, our PHILOSOPHY may say, "I BE-LIEVE in PEOPLE being DETERMINED – of People being SUBJECT to the Laws of the Universe": and at the SAME time, our WORDS are CONTRADICTING this; our WORDS are saying, in ALMOST EVERY UTTERANCE, that this or that ASPECT of a Person is GOVERNED by FREE WILL.

Chapter Eight

DO We Need to PICK Better Words to Use?

Or Are Our Dictionaries Utterly Lacking in Words to Even SELECT From?

Is our view of what words to use, regarding People, rather like being Overweight?

For, to simply SAY that our "PROBLEM" – our "DIAGNOSIS" – is "BEING OVERWEIGHT", hardly SOLVES it, does it?

Neither does a supposed CURE, of "EAT LESS"!

And, "Come back in a month", and we'll see how you are doing."

For. is there any iron-clad, useful, DISCUS-SION of HOW to STOP overeating, or to even define what overeating MEANS?

***

PERHAPS, the ENTIRETY of our "problem", when it comes to speaking or thinking WELL, or even "WELL-ENOUGH", is NOT a problem of "picking the INCORRECT" words, or thus, NOT DELIVERING OUR "LINES" well, but something ENTIRELY DIFFERENT:

Perhaps the TRUE issue is, that what we HAVE, in our "LARDER", our TOOLKIT, to SELECT

FROM, when it comes to our WORDS, is quite
PROBLEMATIC:

Especially when it comes to COMMUNICAT-
ING with words we find utilized in WRITTEN
communications, vs words that originated and are
still used EXCLUSIVELY in people who READ
LITTLE, and use ORALLY-Based words, something less and less commonly found in PURE
form.

Chapter Nine

Is a DETERMINISTIC View of Our Lives Impossible to Deal With?

Now, some will say that it is only Free Will that gives us HOPE, in life....

And thus, that Mankind cannot Handle, a world in which he or she is a cork on the top of a stream....

that this is too "depressing", too "Anti-Hope" to live by.

***

But what if having a GOAL, or a VIEW-POINT on ourselves or others, which is BASED upon FREE WILL, might initially be PLEASUR-ABLE, for a WHILE, but NOT in the MID- or LONG-term?

For what happens, when an INFEASIBLE goal is UNMET, and we then feel DESPONDENT? When our UNFOUNDED Hopes are DASHED, thus, by the matter of what is called REALITY?

And too, what happens, when our UNRE-ALISTIC – our FREE-WILL-Based – GOALS tied to OTHERS, and ourselves, CANNOT be FULFILLED? Doesn't THIS inevitably cause ANGER, and what is called BLAMING? Blaming, in the sense of, "You SHOULD have been ABLE to DO or BE something ELSE, by FREE WILL!"

Or thus, "SHAME on YOU and MYSELF, for NOT being a MAGICIAN that can FLOUT the LAWS of the UNIVERSE, by FREE WILL?"

Chapter Ten

Do Our DICTIONARY-Based People-Words Follow the Laws of the Universe?

If NOT, Are They UN-SCIENTIFIC (Arguably IRRATIONAL)?

I F, thus, we are to see People, in their DE-TAILS, as GOVERNED by LAWS of the UNIVERSE, hence, DETERMINED by such, ought not our WORDS MATCH this OVER-ALL view?

***

For, if we SAY that People – ourselves included – have LIMITATIONS – but our WORDS say the OPPOSITE, this is a PROBLEM, isn't it? More than a SMALL problem: a BIG problem!

***

It seems, thus, like saying, "I BELIEVE that, to LOSE WEIGHT, I need to STOP EATING a

GALLON of ICE CREAM a day, but then, they NEGATE, as per the ACTING upon such:

By failing to PROPERLY DEFINE what an unsuitable AMOUNT of ice cream IS, and instead, saying that the GALLON of ice cream is "MERELY a GALLON of WATER".

Chapter Eleven

Science is Surely Not Just a METHOD of INVESTIGATION, but a SET of TOOLS Which Are RATIONAL

Rational Tools Follow the RATIONALE of the UNIVERSE – That CAUSE AND EFFECT EXISTS

So, if we SAY we believe in DETERMINISM, or even, "Being 'Scientific'", about PEOPLE, not just INANIMATE "Items", and yet, are then NEGATING this OVERALL statement by the USE of TERMS that DEFINE various ASPECTS of People in FREE WILL manner, are we truly WALKING the TALK, as a species?

And if we CLAIM to be People of SCIENCE, but our WORDS are saying that we believe in MAGIC SPELLS and MAGIC WANDS, is THIS very SCIENTIFIC?

***

Indeed, IF someone were to say, I am BET-TER than YOU are, as a Person, overall, or in my THINKING, because I am "SCIENTIFIC", while YOU believe in GHOSTS and HOB-GOBLINS, and yet, our WORDS are VIEWING People in the same GHOST- and HOB-GOBLIN MAN-NER, a manner that IGNORES the REALITY of DETERMINISM, is this any the LESS "IRRA-TIONAL"? Any the LESS "UNSCIENTIFIC"?

Put another way, the SCIENTIST can have a CLIPBOARD chock FULL of WRITINGS, but if the WRITINGS are full of IRRATIONAL WORDS, called FREE-WILL People-Words, is THIS SCIENCE, and does this person thus QUALIFY to be CALLED a Scientist? For, even a bevy of experiments, and double-blind studies, and test tubes, if LABELED with IRRATIONAL WORDS, is hardly RATIONAL, and thus, hardly SCIENCE, is it?

Chapter Twelve

Do We Humans NEED a Free Will View to Be Happiest?

And is Free Will Thus a BIOLOGICAL NECESSITY for HUMANS?

Now, what of those who claim that to see ourselves and others in FREE WILL fashion, is simply a matter of GENETICS?

IS THIS TRUE?

Likewise, while many would experience great PLEASURE from using Crack Cocaine, does THIS mean, that we are best off UTILIZING Crack?

Or is Crack being utilized as a DRUG, as a CRUTCH, some might say? Especially in periods of high stress, high PAIN?

Chapter Thirteen

Is Over-Indulging in Free-Will-Based Words any DIFFERENT Than any OTHER Coping Mechanism?

Yes, to repeat:

> Is "excessive" "use" of **FREE WILL**, al-
> though **COMFORTING**, in **TIMES** of
> **HIGH STRESS**, something any **DIFFER-**
> **ENT**, than turning to Crack Cocaine, or
> excessive use of **ALCOHOL**, or **METH**, or
> **GAMBLING** - usage?

Or even, excessive dining upon a THANKS-GIVING "spread" of delicious, high-calorie FOOD?

Chapter Fourteen

The Crucial Question: Are Free-Will Words Mostly WISHFUL THINKING?

Or is MOST Free-Will "Viewing" ULTIMATELY a Matter of the WISHES of FREE-WILL SALESMEN?

Now, next: there is a key issue to be addressed, I believe:

***

To what extent do we succumb to a short-term way of dealing with something, a short-term expedient, because of OURSELVES ONLY?

In other words, are we succumbing to a "crutch", out of it seemingly being The Best Way, all in OUR purview?

***

Or are we being UNDULY INFLUENCED by OTHERS, to "engage" in the use of this or that COPING Method?

Put another way, are we often being unduly SWAYED by our OUTER environment, not just our INNER environment?

Are we being unduly influenced by exposure, unwittingly, to a "BAD CROWD" of "People"/influences?

***

I bring this up, because Napoleon Hill (the author of "Think and Grow Rich"), had said, in another book of his, "How to Own Your Own Mind", that we humans need to be aware of just how prone we are, to Wishful Thinking.

***

To WHAT extent, though, is the over-use of a Free Will view – a MAGICAL THINKING point of view – a matter solely of WISHFUL THINK-ING gone AMUK, vs there being OUTSIDE in-fluences which push us strongly?

Likewise, who might not over-indulge in the ar-eas of eating or smoking or drinking alcohol, IF there were not such strong MARKETING for such, either EXPLICITLY, in terms of outright MEDIA ADS, but also, the ADS wherein such PRODUCTS are POSITIONED for "VIEW-ING", that it is almost LITERALLY IMPOS-SIBLE to NOT STUMBLE ALL OVER these items, as one literally drives down the road, or even walks? As one goes to work or is AT work; or as one eats a meal, outside of one's home?

Are these ADS, these MARKETINGS, as per WHERE the products – or IDEAS, too – are PO-SITIONED, and HOW MANY of them, per day – a FACTOR that is GOING BEYOND our CA-PACITY to COPE with?

Are these "ADS", not always VERBAL but "POSITIONAL" by way of how HARD it is to AVOID SEEING them, in our DAILY AC-TIVITIES, an undue influence which is SUPER-SCEDING mere periods of SELF-INDULGING in some "coping method", or as Napoleon Hill also says, WISHFUL THINKING, as a coping method?

***

Hence, just HOW MUCH are we GOV-ERNED by periods, under stress, by WISHFUL THINKING:

Including FREE WILL, and FREE WILL WORD-usage?

Vs how much are we governed by influences from OUTSIDE of ourselves, and this, then NOT a matter of WISHFUL thinking, but THINKING from INUNDATING OUTSIDE elements?

***

Yes, how MUCH is the indulgence in "MAGICAL Thinking" a matter of what WE want to do, vs a response to OUTSIDE influences, call it MARKETING Influences, if you will?

Likewise, there is the phrase, "Birds of a Feather, Flock Together".

And, if someone goes to rehab, they are urged to part ways with influences that could all too easily suck them right back to "using": they are urged to part ways with friends who still "use", and perhaps move out a neighborhood where many are indulging so.

This then goes way beyond simply saying that a former "addict" needs to account for their using only as a matter of their OWN Wishful Thinking, and to take a hard look at how their EXTERNAL environment was and could still be MARKET-ING a way of life that is too much to not succumb to.

THIS concept may be very KINGPIN, hence, in looking at the claims of some, that we would, as a species, COLLAPSE in HOPELESSNESS, if not for the option to turn to FREE WILL for HOPE.

For perhaps SOMETIMES, Free Will views are COMFORTING, and for a PERIOD of time; but many or most might not "indulge" in such Wishful Thinking CHRONICALLY, if not for strong, strong, strong "MARKETING", OF such?

AGAIN, can a former rehab attendee, be expected to be able to NOT SUCCUMB to the CONSTANT "MARKETING" of former addict-friends, or of a addict-populated neighborhood, in general?

Even amongst the "strongest", it would surely require too much Note Taking and Reviewing, in general, to constantly do "cognitive therapy" on such matters; it would consume too many "resources". It would be a MOST INEFFICIENT EXPENDITURE of RESOURCES, overall.

Chapter Fifteen

Free Will and its Free Will WORDS: a PRODUCT Offered to Us?

Are Free Will and Its Words, Marketed Like Alcohol and Cigarettes and Tranquilizers?

I would put it yet another way:

If overuse of ALCOHOL, say, is TEMPT-ING ENOUGH, already, for some, would it be

HELPFUL, to find ourselves subject to the IN-FLUENCE of MARKETING of Alcohol usage, via "billboards", every two feet as we travel down the road, wherever we go?

SIMILARLY, if overindulging in a FREE WILL view is a myopic and short-term EXPEDIENT view of People and People-Matters, does it HELP us any, to have Free Will "MARKETED" to us, too?

Isn't the TEMPTATION of overindulging in Magical Thinking, great enough, ALREADY, without it being MARKETED to us, FROM WITHOUT, not just from WITHIN, at times?

***

Or put another way, if a 5,000 calorie Thanksgiving Dinner is highly pleasurable, do we BENEFIT by any MARKETING MESSAGES, that to EAT such a high-calorie, and high-cost, item, DAILY, is OPTIMAL?

Does this unduly influence us to go past what we would ordinarily better "handle"?

Does such marketing cause us to go BEYOND pursuing indulging in experiences, and THINK-ING in certain ways, "IN MODERATION"?

Yes, is there STRONG MARKETING, of FREE WILL as applied to PEOPLE – and via the WORDS we have, AT our becken call – that essentially is UNDULY OVERRIDING our INBUILT TENDENCIES toward SELF-COR-RCTING any over-indulgences that could be called STRAYING TOO FAR into NON-MOD-ERATION?

***

Put yet another way: if many of us find it under-standably useful – optimal – to "TAKE a BREAK"

- a "VACATION", at times – does this mean it is then ALSO good – optimal – to "take a break", every hour, every day, to thus OVER-INDULGE in such "breaks", even such "blowing off steam"?

Is this a problem the AVERAGE person HAS, IN-BUILT, as per "WISHFUL THINKING", or an "ADDICTIVE MINDSET"?

Or is it almost NON-HUMAN, to RESIST too much MARKETING? Of ANYTHING?

***

In fact, most people would NOT INDULGE in literally JUMPING OUT of a WINDOW, when the "going gets tough", as a few did, during the Great Depression in the 1930s; yet, IF a person were TOLD, not by SELF-Talk Marketing, by MARKETING by the talk of some OUTSIDE

MARKETERS, that one OUGHT to jump out of that window, and one were TOLD such marketing messages EVERY TEN SECONDS, for DAYS and WEEKS and YEARS, might MANY people OPEN up that window and JUMP?

***

By the way, a sales book I was reading, yesterday, was claiming that the average person buys a product only after being told of it, SEVEN TIMES.

(Or, in other words, because the PRODUCT – or IDEA – was MARKETED to them – SEVEN TIMES.)

HENCE, it was the REPETITIVE MARKETING MESSAGE which had THE SWAY, NOT, perhaps, the supposed necessity of it TAKING seven times to ADEQUATELY EXPLAIN any and all MERITS of the product.

You COULD say, in fact, that a young child who MARKETS to their PARENTS, for a NEW, EXPENSIVE BICYCLE or ELECTRONIC gadget, might well OBTAIN such an item; NOT because the child's constant marketing provided enough LOGIC to CONVINCE the parents; but instead, because the barrage of marketing simply WORE DOWN the parents' RESERVES to DEAL with such.

Hence, the parents did not have, often, a DESIRE, BUILT-IN, to buy the item, but rather, they succumbed to the child's REPETITIVE MARKETING messages.

Chapter Sixteen

Can FREE WILL and DETERMINISM CO-EXIST?

What is the PAYOFF of Claiming That Free Will and Determinism Both Exist Side by Side?

One final matter:

SOME say that both FREE WILL and DETERMINISM can and do CO-EXIST.

But IS this TRUE?

CAN one be both PREGNANT and NOT Pregnant, or both ALIVE and NOT Alive?

***

And furthermore, what is the PAYOFF, to someone, of saying or believing this?

I see a rather "unconscious" benefit playing out, in some people who have this viewpoint: I refer to it as the use of what I have coined,

The FREE WILL/DETERMINISM FLIP-FLOP:

Wherein a person DOES believe in both Free Will and Determinism, as co-existing:

But NOT in the SAME PERSON.

For they appear to believe, in a FLIP-FLOP fash-ion, depending on WHOM is being TALKED about:

That issues with the person are EITHER – and only – a matter of FREE WILL – or else, of DE-TERMINISM:

That basically, THEIR "flaws" are a matter of an UTTERLY EXPLAINED, and WELL-ADVO-CATED-for, lineup of a CHAIN OF EVENTS, in other words, of DETERMINED aspects.

Hence, they BELIEVE in ALL OF the NEG-ATIVE aspects, of THEM-selves, as DETER-MINED: that such LOGICALLY, thus, could NOT have been ANY OTHER WAY.

Or as some have touted, "All Prisoners be-lieve they are INNOCENT" ... innocent, I might say, of WHATEVER having happened, in their lives, as falling OUTSIDE of the purview of DE-TERMINISM: in other words, that WHAT TRANSPIRED, HAPPENED so, because of a clear CHAIN of EVENTS that was thus IN-

EVITABLE; and what is INEVITABLE cannot TECHNICALLY be a CRIME, but instead, a sort of a "CODE VIOLATION".

***

Yes, it strikes me, that some people see THEIR OWN non-ideal aspects as DETERMINED, but then see OTHERS' "issues" as based upon CHOICE, in other words, FREE WILL.

***

Put yet another way, The Free Will – Determinism Flip-Flop being this:

> "ALL of who I am, is EXPLAINABLE; but, on the OTHER hand, some of what SOME OTHERS are, is NOT explainable – by a chain of events – but instead, BY FREE WILL – by 'CHOICE', hence."

Hence, a QUASI-Belief in both Free Will and Determinism:

ALL of what I AM is DETERMINED; BUT, some of what YOU are, is due to FREE WILL.

How CONVENIENT, we might say....

***

Indeed, although I am not a lawyer, it strikes me, that some lawyers might be highly SKILLED, in ADVOCATING for their CLIENTS, by providing a COGENT, even UTTERLY ACCURATE LIST of the CHAIN of EVENTS related to the matters at hand:

(The quintessential definition of DETERMINISM?)

But when it comes to the OTHER party, this chain of events might be MINIMIZED or IGNORED, even DENIED, as being POSSIBLE.

Indeed, is not the very CONCEPT of ADVOCATING, a list of reasons, based upon a STRING OF CAUSE and EFFECTS?

For if we SEE, clearly, a given CHAIN of EVENTS, who can ARGUE that it COULD have been OTHERWISE?

***

And is not this, the ESSENCE of DETERMIN-ISM?

And might a highly SKILLED person, whether a LAWYER or not, technically speaking, is surely TRYING to lay out a LOGICAL ARGUMENT for a certain viewpoint: a CHAIN-Of-Events-Based viewpoint, if you will:

Which is the ESSENCE of the PHILOSOPHI-CAL concept of DETERMINISM, or moreover, WHAT WE CALL "COMMON SENSE", even?

In other words, a skilled lawyer presents "REA-SONS", in logical order, for EVERYTHING": or more accurately stated, perhaps, that there "IS a SET of Reasons, in LOGICAL ORDER, for everything: a RECIPE, if you will, that MAKES not only PIES, CAKES, MEAT dishes, as "OUT-

COMES" at a certain point, but for EVERY AS-PECT in HUMAN BEINGS' lives, too. That humans are NO EXCEPTION: that we ARE, thus, WHATEVER WENT INTO us, and whatever, too, the CONSTRAINTS were.

So, for the baking of a CAKE, the INGREDI-ENTS were flour, sugar, and spices; and the CON-STRAINTS were the TEMPERATURE of the OVEN, and the AMOUNT of TIME that the HEAT was "APPLIED" to the Ingredients.

One last comment: if one puts in flour and sug-ar and spices, into a container, and applies heat for a certain amount of time, NO AMOUNT, WHATSOEVER, of FREE-WILL-based WISH-FUL THINKING, would EVER come out as a TREE, or a DUCK, or a ROCK.

And thus, too, an ACORN will only grow into a certain TYPE of TREE; not a LAKE or CAR or WHATEVER ELSE we might DESIRE (wish) it to.

Period.

General Comments...

This writing has "fingerprints" and other blemishes...

This "item" may appear rather simple in layout and length, but might I mention that it took years upon years to come to the ideas herein? An almost utterly unbelievable amount of resources have found their way to what follows.

I have come to these ideas in stages. And then often worked and re-worked them, as I then sought to address various contradictions. Or call such, "discrepancy-solvings". To include, why isn't there much out in print, on the nuances presented in this book to follow?

Why, too, are our ideas on words so lopsided, hence?

***

The book may lack polish and marketing, too, but surely there are always reasons why we find our resources allocated as they are. Suffice it to say, that I have a lot on my plate, these days, and so, lack the resources for air-brushing.

There is no attempt being made to air-brush the words or sentence-structures, to a 3rd-grade level, also.

I'm not at all sure that would be in anyone's best interest.

My "recognition", hence, for any cumbersome delivery. The polishing up of such "cosmetics" and ease of use, would mean that this would never be written....

Likewise, if we attended an outdoor sporting event only if the venue provider could guarantee that we encounter no rain, and too, that the temperature would be within two degrees of our favorite temperature, and too, that there would be no traffic on the roads, we would never find ourselves attending such an event: the provider of such an event would be spending far too many resources on "cosmetics", for what they have in their larder of "tools".

I have read about and thought for myself, on the topics in this "item" for my entire life.

It is a melding of what one sees and is told. And an attempt to patiently sift through Mankind's craving to believe we have The Answers. I too surely am missing something here and there, also, but one thing I think I can say, is that being impatient in delivering something I know to be "full of holes", is not exactly what went into my upbringing, my "training"....

So, at the age of sixty-three, now, I am presenting this and other ideas of mine, when I believe that further refining is not going to produce much more for any of us to benefit by, in the overall scheme of life.

***

Might we consider, thus, the following? And perhaps this explains why I have spent decades "sitting on" so many of my ideas, seeking to eliminate – solve – as many discrepancies as I possibly can:

***

A famous poem — "The Blind Men and the Elephant" by John Godfrey Saxe (1816–1887), talks of how we all see things somewhat differently:

"And so these men of Hindustan

Disputed loud and long,

Each in his own opinion

Exceeding stiff and strong,

Though each was partly in the right

And all were in the wrong.

***

The poem begins:

It was six men of In-

dostan

To learning much
inclined,

Who went to see the
Elephant

(Though all of
them were blind),

That each by obser-
vation

Might satisfy his
mind.

They conclude that the elephant is like a wall,
snake, spear, tree, fan or rope, depending upon

where they touch. None of blind men's descrip-
tion is correct for the whole elephant."

https://simple.wikipedia.org/wiki/Blind_men_
and_an_elephant

About the author

Mother, left; grandmother who raised the author his first four years in waking hours, middle; helper, right. Poland, 1940, before mother and grandmother emigrated to America in 1950

Contact information:

message@goldpogo.com

This Author's "Training"...

This book is not written by someone with Conventional Training in Linguistics. IF some are referring to training as a Program of Instruction, garnered from a Brick-and-Mortar Organization.

Perhaps, too, there is a tremendously different view of what is meant by Conventional Training, depending upon both geographical location within any particular country, and the degree of reading that one does or doesn't do.

Indeed, this author hypothesizes that there is a vast difference in the TYPE of words utilized, by human beings, and that these fall into two groups:

words found in books, vs words found only in what could be called Orally-collected-and-used words.

The author would further hypothesize that what makes the areas of music, art, dance, and the concepts of Intuition and Autodidact Training, at times, and the Buddhist concept of Thinking Less, and Mindfulness Meditation, and "Saying Less Can be Saying More", have a tremendous amount to do with any and all forms of thinking that do not utilize "Book-Based-Words", with some arguably key limitations.

***

The author may have a rather uncommon Training of sorts, when it comes to some areas in life, including the topic of linguistics, aka Words:

First, he was raised by his grandmother, during most of his waking hours of his first four years of his life.

What makes this of particular mention, though, is that she spoke no English, but German: born and raised in a hamlet in Poland, they spoke German in that region.

Now, for some reason, she made no attempt to speak German to her grandson – this author. Perhaps his parents had asked her not to. At any rate, he grew up hearing almost no German or English or any other language spoken to him, those first four years, compared to most children in general.

Their first significant conversation – in English thus – was when the author was thirty.

Next, his grandmother had read from parts of only one or two books during her entire lifetime: the Bible being one of these.

Thirdly, she was a farmer and mother – of six children – her whole life. She left the farm only a couple of times a week, for grocery shopping and to go to an ethnic church, where German was spoken, and everyone there spoke German and "broken" English. She rarely ever ate in restaurants, rarely went to movies, and never drove a car during her lifetime.

Fourthly, her husband, born in Ukraine, also rarely read any books. Both had minimal amounts of schooling, perhaps sixth- grade level at most.

***

Some other factors also had sway, perhaps:

The author took a year off, after Kindergarten, and spent most of that time in the woods of North Carolina, walking, collecting leaves, rocks, turtles, and observing in general.

A few years later, he was frequently walking, on the extensive wooded lands of St. Thomas More

Catholic School, near where his father was attending graduate school.

Also, the author and his parents had moved very frequently, in his earlier years of life: by the time he had graduated from high school, they had moved ten times.

Another factor: from the age of twelve until sixteen, he essentially had his own living quarters, and rarely spent time with his parents, except for a half-hour each evening, for dinner:

***

He essentially had a separate apartment from the rest of his biological family of two parents and his sister: they were on the top part of the split-level home, and he occupied the entire bottom half, complete with kitchenette, shower, study room, adjustable thermostat, bedroom, and weightlifting room. He also had his own telephone and ham radio setup. This "apartment" had a private entrance/exit.

Additionally, because his parents had originally been of the Christian denomination known as the Plymouth Brethren, similar in ways to the Amish and Mennonites – and indeed, his grandmother's husband was a Mennonite – he was permitted to watch only one television show for years: The Waltons. He was also not allowed to dance or attend dances. And because of his being tall and underweight, he was not exactly top draw in "looks". Also add in, eyeglasses and a lisp, with speech therapy for years and years. And too, his frail build meant that he never took up sports, before graduating from high school.

This home was on a sizeable lake, in a village of 2,000, in Minnesota, at the end of a short road, which connected with no other roads, too.

Now, for company, his friends tended to be adults: adults who often were smart, but had not done much people-based reading, compared to many persons: one, a ninth-grade mathematics teacher of his, took him under his wing: each day for a year, when fourteen, he would help the sixty-year-old mathematics teacher, a fellow ham radio operator, clean up the classroom.

***

Indeed, his frailty was enough of an issue, that when he found himself at West Point, studying pre-med, he was put on dining tables with the West Point football team players, to provide him with double rations of food that the football players received. He was also directed to take up the "intramural sport" of weightlifting, during the second half of his first year there: with the football team, again, as co-weightlifters.

What he lacked in muscles, he was compensating for in other areas:

When his grades in boxing and gymnastics – D's – were a hindrance to his pursuits of medicine – he changed his course of study to electrical engineering – considered the most difficult course of study there at West Point, to take up.

And after lights out, at 11:00 in the evening, and his roommates had gone to bed, he turned on his study light, again, and wrote in journals and read, typically until 1:30 into the morning. And then, up at 5:00 a.m. for mandatory breakfast soon thereafter. Saturday afternoons were sleep catch-up time, while most other cadets were at football and other games. He never attended any football games, thus, other than the Army-Navy games.

Yet other influences in the area of Words, were the influences of his mother and father, in the arts and writing: his mother loved to do craftwork, calligraphy, and gardening; she also put in immense work in helping him train in the area of playing the violin, to include innumerable hours involved with his Suzuki violin time, at the McPhail Center for Music, in Minneapolis. His father also had great influence, what with being an English instructor – English literature – at many a college, over the years; his father also introduced him to photography when seven. And his father also spent immense time helping him in his Senior year of high school, with the development of his writing skills. He also funded violin training over the years, including private lessons with a private instructor at a nearby college: a Mr. John Lindsey, who interestingly had once attended the premiere civil engineering school in the nation, before switching his major to music: he brought strong rigor to the author's violin training, thus. Violin was practiced seven days a week, two hours a day, and with each Saturday and Sunday sandwiching in a violin lesson and an orchestra session.

There is also the reality of never having married or having had children, although he had had four long-term relationships, one of which involved being engaged for two years. this provided lots of time, but at a "cost" – for the intellect, to include lots and lots of time spent on developing new words, word theory, and writing, in general.

It also meant having the time to attend Berea College at the half-time level, and study fifteen mathematics classes there, starting at the age of 41; and to start using SuperMemo, a software program, too, which he utilized to accrue 160,000 flashcards in various facets of Mankind – aka People. And to work on his photography.

Refund policy

Refund information:

If for any reason, you find this item not quite your
cup of tea, I am most happy to provide a refund,
no questions asked.

One can contact me at message@goldpogo.com.

Or, one can write me at this address, asking for a
refund:

Loran Joly

Box # 1036

1303 US 127 South

Suite 104

Frankfort, KY 40601

9 798869 350794